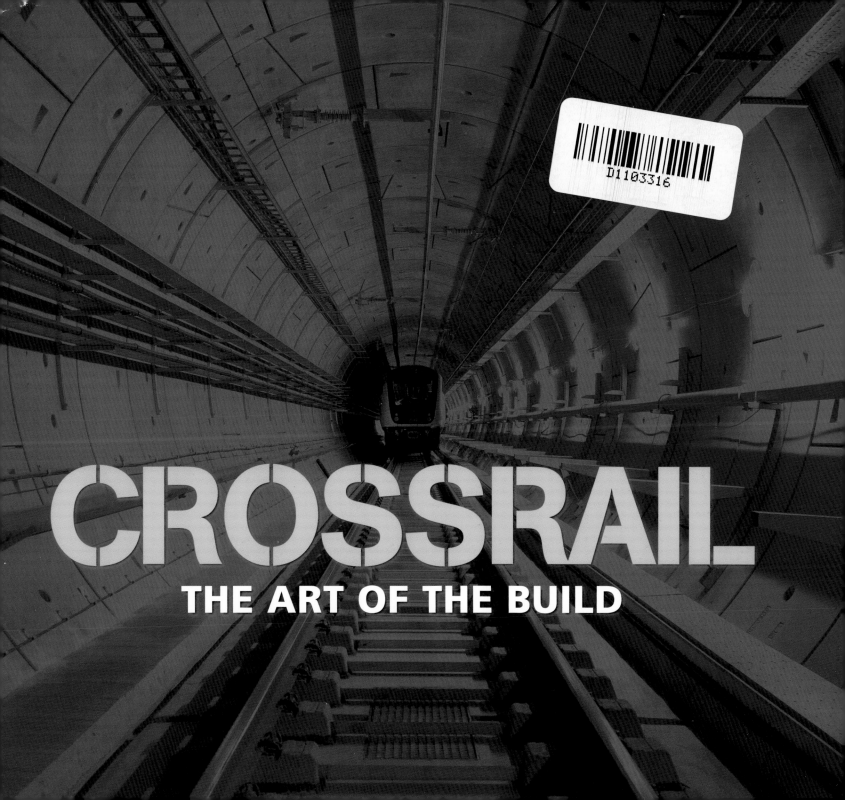

CROSSRAIL

THE ART OF THE BUILD

Crossrail: The Art of the Build

This edition published in the United Kingdom in 2018
by Crossrail Limited: 25 Canada Square,
Canary Wharf, London, E14 5LQ.

Text © Crossrail Limited 2018
Design & Layout © Crossrail Limited 2018

ISBN 978-0-9933433-3-9

Editor: Sarah Allen
Contributors: Julian Glover, Hugh Pearman,
Louisa Buck, Tony Travers
Creative direction & design: Andrew Briffett

With additional contributions from
Crossrail and its partners.

Crossrail Limited is registered in England and Wales
No. 4212657.

Registered Office:
25 Canada Square, Canary Wharf, London, E14 5LQ.

Cover image by Dan Garrity

CROSSRAIL

THE ART OF THE BUILD

Foreword

Simon Wright OBE
Chief Executive & Programme Director

By 2030 the capital's population is set to reach 10 million and its transport system must be ready to meet this demand. The Elizabeth line is part of this plan. The Crossrail project is delivering the new railway to provide a 10% increase in capacity in central London and help maintain London's place as a global city.

The new railway will be a high frequency, high capacity service linking 41 stations over 100 kilometres from Reading and Heathrow in the west, through central London, to Shenfield and Abbey Wood in the east. It will give 1.5 million additional people access to central London within 45 minutes, reduce journey times and offer a world class customer experience.

The project required 42 kilometres of new tunnels, 10 new stations, over 50 kilometres of new track, integration of three signalling systems and upgrades across existing infrastructure.

A large integrated team has been essential to delivering Crossrail. The project has needed the very best expertise in civil engineering, design, systems technology and operations to deliver the build and prepare for live railway operations. I would like to thank to each and every member of the team who has contributed to the project and the stakeholders who have supported us throughout.

This book presents the reflections of four writers, specialists in history, architecture, art and economics, on the Crossrail project and the future Elizabeth line. It reflects on Crossrail's place in the history of rail development, its contribution to the built environment, the exceptional public art being delivered at new stations and its impact on the city. These articles underline the scale of the project and its importance to London and the UK.

The Crossrail project is in its final stages – the Elizabeth line is coming.

Foreword

Sir Terry Morgan CBE
Chairman

Crossrail has been an infrastructure project of huge ambition. Committing to the project was an expression of great confidence in the skills and ability of the UK's construction industry. Its delivery will be a significant boost to the UK, signifying the country's commitment to growth.

When the railway was conceived – many decades ago – it was planned to increase capacity in central London, improve journeys and open up opportunity for people living along the route and beyond. With the railway now running with new trains on the east and west of the route, and the central section due to open in December 2018, the Elizabeth line will more than deliver on this promise. By December 2019 the railway will integrate services throughout the route and the UK will have a state-of-the-art new railway to be proud of.

New stations and urban realm schemes around them will become new local landmarks. World class public art installations within them will enhance the experience for people as they travel. New homes are being delivered all along the new corridor and commercial developments will offer new offices, retail and entertainment venues to the UK.

During construction, the project has been able to make a contribution quite distinct from the future railway. Crossrail

has supported 55,000 jobs all around the UK. It has trained a new generation in underground construction skills through its academy. It has increased the number of young people entering the industry, recruiting over 1,000 apprentices, and it has driven up health and safety standards. It has engaged people around the world by opening up its story of construction, archaeology, design and delivery.

Crossrail is being delivered through a collaborative, partnership approach bringing together many parties. The project has been funded by the Department for Transport and Transport for London, with contributions from London's businesses and commercial partners. The project's delivery has been through an integrated team, including our Project Delivery Partner Bechtel, to whom I give my particular thanks. The art programme has been funded by corporate sponsors and the City of London. The patience and support of stakeholders and the people affected during construction works has been a foundation on which we have been able to deliver. With this in mind it seems a whole generation of people in the UK have a stake in the project and can share our pride in seeing it delivered as we look ahead to the launch of the Elizabeth line in December 2018.

SETTING THE CONTEXT

Julian Glover

A map of London's history would start with its rivers and bridges, edge out from its Roman and medieval core and then show a place transformed by its railways. The million-strong city which existed in 1801, before the trains came, though huge by world standards and very congested, was still walkable. There were fields within reach in every direction. The city which dominated Britain a century later, six times as populous and more than that in extent, was one only the railways could make work.

Modern London has been shaped by its trains – and their development has, in turn, been led by the demands of the city. It has always led the way. In 1836 London was the first capital to be served by a train. In 1863 it was the first to open an underground passenger railway. In the years which followed it invented the deep Tube, commuter railways, the modern metro map and, on the Victoria line in 1968, automated operation.

The Elizabeth line is the latest advance, but its history is also part of the story of the early pioneers. Heading west, the new trains reach stations such as Ealing Broadway which has been welcoming passengers since 1838, less than a decade after the first steam passenger trains anywhere began running between Liverpool and Manchester. To the east they will call at Ilford, which originally opened only a year later.

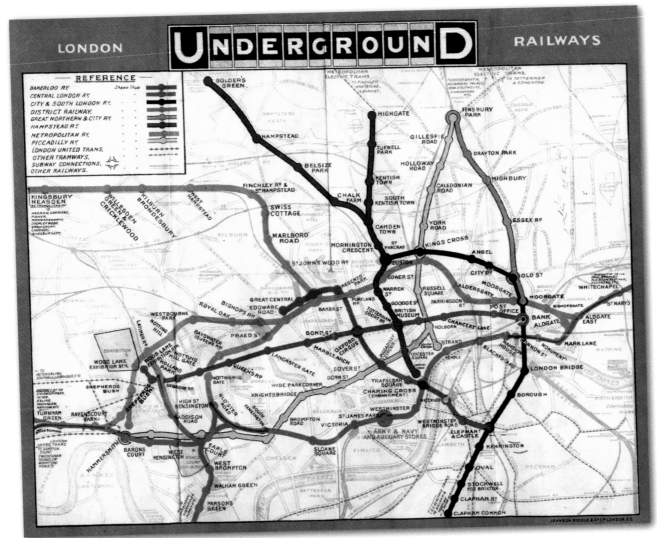

London Tube map, circa 1908.

When the early trains came these suburbs were only fields and farmhouses: Ilford was home to only 10,000 people as late as 1891 and Shenfield station, also on the future Elizabeth line, was shut down for a time after 1850 because so few people used it. The Great Western Railway was slow to give Ealing a frequent or affordable service. When it finally did, in the 1890s, the growth which followed was explosive. The population tripled in thirty years and it has kept on growing.

Today it is the Elizabeth line's new routes which are powering the building of new homes but the recipe is the same: a need for places to live and an easy way to travel, with frequent services and simple fares. "The railways have set us all moving far away from London," one surveyor noted in 1871 as commuter services grew.

On each of the rail routes into London you can trace the city's expansion by the style of the trackside houses, interwar semis giving way to Victorian villas and terraces before grinding to a halt at the terminus stations which guard the historic core.

None of this was planned. Elsewhere in Europe the development of railways was largely overseen by the state – if not always run or funded by it. Military planners had a say in the layout and even the track gauges of the railways; so did government rules such as France's Law of 1842 which put the building of the network under official and supposedly rational control. This led, in Germany, to the idea of the unified Hauptbahnhof, in the city centre, where different routes converged.

London – and Britain – was different. Free spirits ruled and the result can be seen today. By 1845 the country had 1,000 miles of mainlines, run by 19 different operators. Brunel's Great Western line to Paddington and Stephenson's route from Birmingham into Euston nearly touch at Old Oak Common, where the Elizabeth line will one day meet High Speed Two. They could easily have shared a central station and the 1835 Act authorising the Great Western assumed that would be the case, with both lines going to Euston, in which case there would have been no Paddington station to call at and no line immediately to the west for the Elizabeth line to use.

But commercial rivalry got the upper hand, as it did for a century. Almost every new route into the city led to a new terminus with the result that London has more than any other city in Europe. This spurred on the city's expansion – all those new lines and stations needed passengers, which encouraged competition and rapid growth. But it also produced a problem which even now London has not managed to solve. A disjointed system poured people into the centre and only made the old problem of congestion worse.

(Top image) Paddington station platforms circa 19th century;

Brunel's engine sheds at Paddington yard;

The 19th century civil engineer; Isambard Kingdom Brunel.

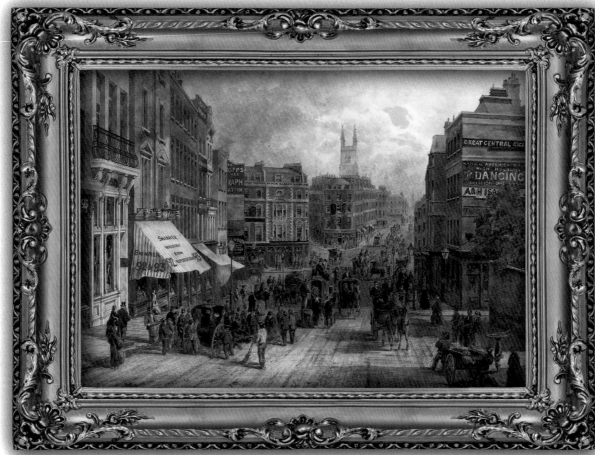

Snow Hill, Holborn, London. English School, 19th Century.

Visitors to London in the great days of railway expansion were shocked by what they found. Visiting the capital for the first time in 1848, Charlotte and Anne Brontë 'became so dismayed by the crowded streets, and the impeded crossings, that they stood still repeatedly'. Promoting plans for a new line to Charing Cross a decade later, on behalf of the South Eastern Railway, the author Samuel Smiles pointed out that, "the journey by cab or omnibus from Paddington to London Bridge occupies the same time as the journey by railway from London Bridge to Tunbridge Wells."

How could this be sorted out? In 1846 a Royal Commission made a rare official intervention into the otherwise undirected growth of the railway network, in a year in which 19 new central London stations were being proposed, like a cancerous disease eating up its host city.

Each new line and big new station benefited those who could afford to use it but the impact on those who lived in the way was shocking, their homes knocked down with little compensation. "A poor man is chained to the spot. He has not leisure to walk and he has not money to ride a distance from his work," the urban reformer Charles Pearson told the Commission in protest.

It ruled that railways should not be built into the heart of the city, which limited the destruction they caused, especially to the wealthier parts of the city, but it did nothing to solve congestion.

Pearson took on the challenge himself. His first proposal was to rationalise the growth of the railways by bringing them together in a new united station. When this proved impracticable he pressed on with a second, transformative idea: an underground passenger railway which could carry people reliably between mainline stations beneath streets clogged with horses and carriages.

The first section of Pearson's Metropolitan Railway, from Paddington to Farringdon, opened in 1863, just after his death. It was the direct ancestor not just of the Tube and every metro system in the world but also of the Crossrail project and the future Elizabeth line. It is no accident that London's newest high-capacity underground line serves the stations which stood at either end of its oldest. Both are intended to keep people moving when they reach the end of the original overground routes into London; Crossrail tunnels run on, like the Metropolitan line which opened in 1874, from Farringdon to Liverpool Street and beyond.

(Above) Advertisement for the designs of the Metropolitian line stations.
(left) Urban reformer;
Charles Pearson, circa 1855.

Not all the main lines into London welcomed the mass of people who soon used them to travel into and about the city. The grand trunk routes to the north and west, in particular, put freight and long-distance travellers first, and had to be goaded by law and by the London County Council to run reasonable and affordable services for workers. Others – such as lines to Kent and the north-east of London, where there was less prime profitable traffic, encouraged their local trade. This, in turn, directed the spread of the Victorian city with tight streets of affordable housing in places such as Peckham where cheap travel to the city was most available.

Elsewhere it was not until the twentieth century that new services, especially on the electric Tube, saw houses built on fields. The opening of Golders Green, now on the Northern line, in 1907, was followed by rapid urbanisation which continued in the interwar years as the electric Tube's reach extended to the north. The Metropolitan Railway expanded its services into what became famous as Metro-Land. It fought to the last as a profitable private operator until it was incorporated into state-run London Transport in 1933.

(Far right) Golders Green station in 1906. (right) A guide to Metro-Land published in 1921.

Victoria line train standing in the platform at South Ealing station, circa 1970.

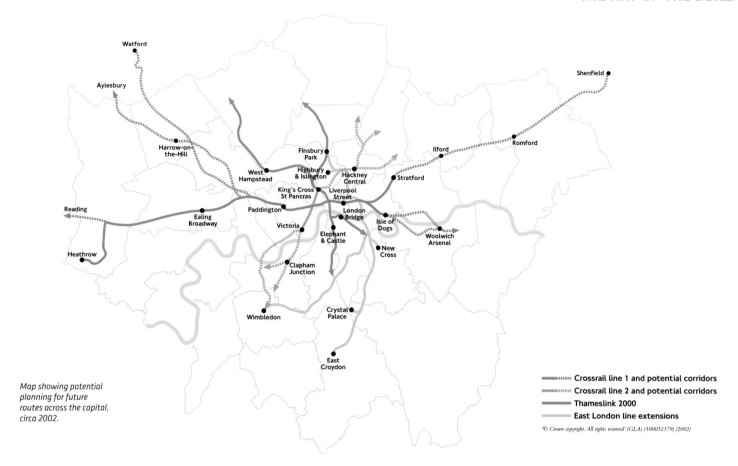

Map showing potential planning for future routes across the capital, circa 2002.

Crossrail line 1 and potential corridors
Crossrail line 2 and potential corridors
Thameslink 2000
East London line extensions

That marked the moment the development of London's railways and suburbs came under strategic direction, though some plans, such as the full expansion of the Northern line, were left uncompleted after the Second World War, which is why today you cannot catch a Tube to Alexandra Palace or Muswell Hill. The challenge in the years that followed was less drawing up good plans than finding the money to implement them.

The 1944 Abercrombie Plan on urban development proposed two east-west Tube lines, which never happened. A few years later the Victoria line was at least built, but funding constraints can still be felt by passengers in the restricted passageways and few, congested escalators which serve it

– errors put right when the Jubilee line extension was built in the 1990s and in spacious new Elizabeth line stations today.

It took the far-thinking 1974 London Rail Study to come up with the name for the new line – CrossRail – and to propose it should carry mainline trains under London, not just smaller Tube carriages. In 1989 the Central London Rail study endorsed the route but it was another twenty years before funding was finally found and building could start.

Charles Pearson, who fought so hard to get the first Metropolitan line built, would have recognised both the challenges of congestion and why, in the end, only a new underground railway can solve them.

The urban realm roof
garden at Canary
Wharf station.

LONDON'S NEW
CIVIC REALM

Hugh Pearman

There is a new civic realm to be explored, from street level to deep under ground, woven tightly into the fabric of London and stretching far beyond. These are the movement-places of the Elizabeth line, threaded through the existing layers of the city and rising to the surface east and west of it. If you thought that this new railway is all about tunnels and trains, that is only part of the picture. It is about speed, yes – with faster trains and more widely-spaced stations than a Tube line, it is more like the RER system in Paris – but also numbers. When it fully opens as the Elizabeth line it will add 10% to the rail capacity of central London. That fact alone has enormous physical and aesthetic implications for the whole of the capital.

The system is designed for over 200 million passenger journeys a year, with people entering and leaving the system at 41 stations all the way along its length of more than 100 kilometres from Reading in Berkshire and Heathrow Airport to Abbey Wood in southeast London and (via a separate branch) to Shenfield in Essex. Ten of these stations are brand new, including a series of five huge new central London subterranean examples: Paddington, Bond Street, Tottenham Court Road, Farringdon and Liverpool Street. These are not like conventional Underground

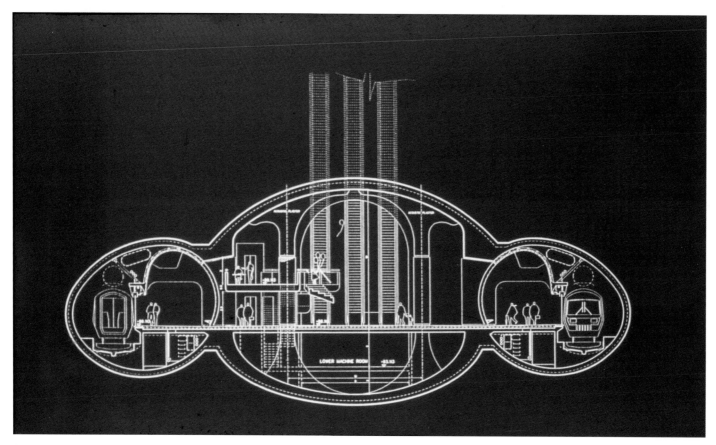

(Above) Early Farringdon station concept design, circa 1990.

stations. Since each mainline train can carry roughly twice as many people as a typical London Underground train, everything is then proportionately scaled up from the trains. The running tunnels between stations, for instance, are more than two and a half metres wider in diameter than existing Tubes such as the Piccadilly or Central lines. The platforms are up to 250 metres long. And all the passenger space is designed to handle concentrated bursts of people, both within the confines of the system and – something that has not happened on the smaller earlier Tube lines – in the streets around the stations,

sometimes affecting the local authorities' public-realm design for a considerable distance. Street improvements, pavement widening, pocket parks, new plazas are part of this while several of the busiest central stations are essentially two stations in one, with widely-separated entrances and exits to diffuse travellers into the townscape evenly.

The consequence of all this is that the spaces we move through, from the surrounding streets via station entrances, through ticket halls to the platforms and onto the trains themselves, are

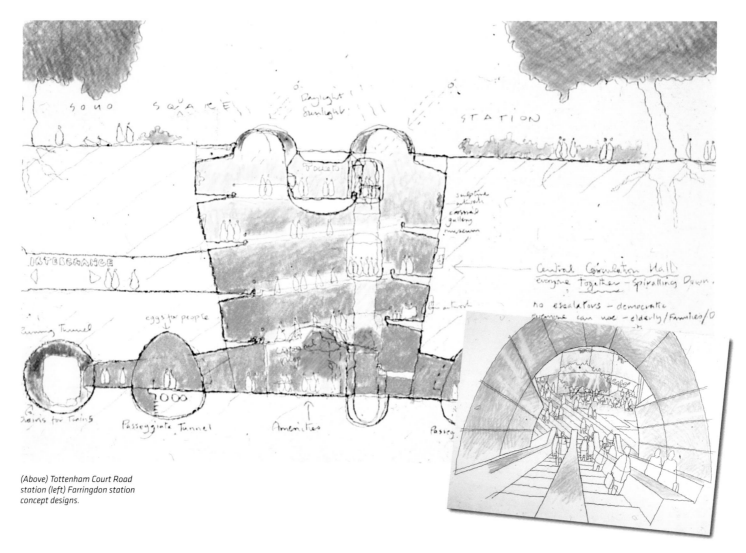

(Above) Tottenham Court Road
station (left) Farringdon station
concept designs.

just grander affairs than most of what we are used to on the London Underground network, parts of which are more than 150 years old. Everything is wider, taller, longer: and designed to last at least a century. This results in some moments of considerable grandeur along the way.

Some of the concept designs for an earlier version of the line, back in the 1980s, proved to be fanciful – there are no chandeliers or tropical glasshouses to be found as originally imagined, for instance. Perhaps even then these ideas were tongue in cheek, but the drawings in the archives show just how much the scale of the operation stimulated the imaginations of the architects and designers. Something of that feeling has however come

The long and wide platforms in the new stations.

through, not only in the engineering and architecture but also in the line's ambitious programme of public art in the central area. In the early days of the planning of the present line, good architecture and design, as opposed to civil engineering, seemed to be almost absent from the thinking – something that caused concern among commentators and the professions. London had become used to the very high design standards of the stations on the Jubilee line extension from Green Park to Stratford, completed just in time for the Millennium. And that was a relatively conventional narrow-bore, standard-capacity Tube line. Could not Crossrail at least aspire to those standards for the Elizabeth line? Did it have to be coldly functional throughout? A rethink took place. Good architects and designers were appointed to work with the engineers, some of them veterans of the earlier project which was ready to go in 1994, but mothballed. When revived, a lot of tweaking to the concept took place. One decisive policy from the earlier exercise remained, however: the notion of contextual design on the surface, differing station by station, even entrance by entrance according to the surroundings and the individual architects: but linked by a common aesthetic below ground with a common kit of component parts. Some of these are also deployed where needed to the stations right along the co-opted surface lines to east and west, where many existing stations are refurbished and expanded.

Farringdon station platform.

From Paddington to Woolwich, under ground is no place for confusion or bottlenecks. The holes dug for these stations are of two kinds – excavated boxes at Paddington, Canary Wharf and Woolwich (in all these cases where the line is relatively close to the surface), and 'mined' stations elsewhere, which are made by tunnelling in the time-honoured way. Except that tunnelling methods have changed. The old system of lining the platform tunnels and passageways with rings of iron or concrete, requiring sharp corners at intersections, has mostly been replaced with the sprayed-concrete method. This has a much more fluid feel to it. Corners are rounded and gentle, passageways are tall. They are lined with curving panels of smooth pale glass-fibre reinforced concrete (GFRC), part-perforated for acoustic absorption. They give the Elizabeth line a very distinct, almost minimalist identity that should not date – the feel of the spaces is such that you will know immediately what line you are on. These linings are then supplemented by special designs of seating, signage, lighting and so forth which minimise visual clutter and are consistent right along the line. Meanwhile the graphics demonstrate the continuing evolution of the long-established and familiar Transport for London principles, with a new identifying colour – purple – for the Elizabeth line.

Elizabeth line
↑ Eastbound platform A
Stratford
Abbey Wood

Elizabeth line
Westbound platform B ↑
← Heathrow
Maidenhead
Reading

A signage totem at Farringdon station.

*Farringdon station's western ticket hall
diamond patterned pre-cast concrete ceiling.*

The light-flooded Tottenham Court Road western ticket hall.

You might think that when you are designing a railway line from scratch you can make everything to exactly the shape, geometry and dimensions that you like. Well, only up to a point. Yes, you can predict the numbers of people likely to use the service, both now and for many decades into the future as London expands – an expansion driven in part by the line itself. You can design for shorter trains at first and longer ones later. You can build in space to add extra escalators in future. But in the congested centre of London, making the interchanges with other lines in the places where they are needed, space is tight even deep under ground, and certainly on the surface. In places existing tunnels are avoided by inches although there is only one station – Tottenham Court Road – where one of the station platforms has to take on a gentle curve to avoid obstacles. And the most congested

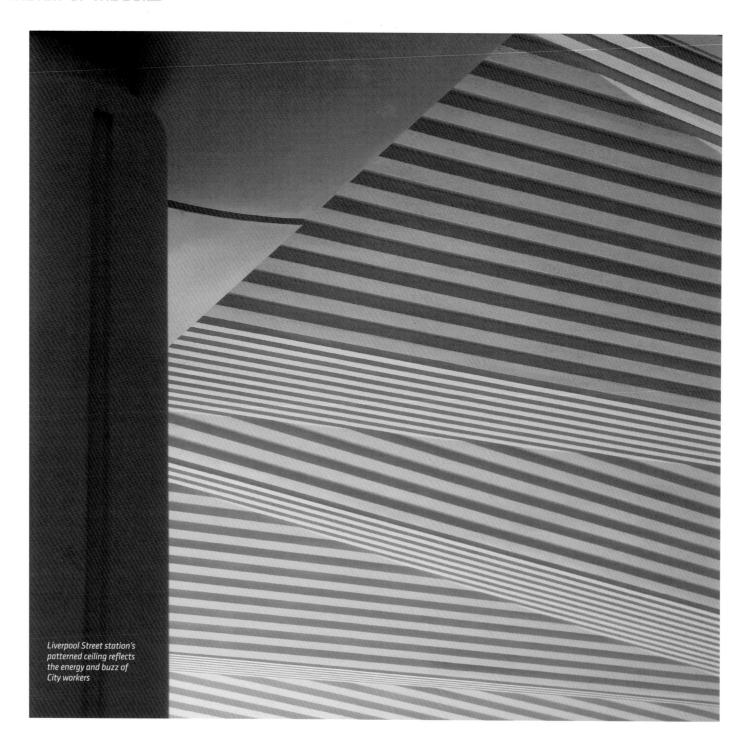

Liverpool Street station's patterned ceiling reflects the energy and buzz of City workers

*Liverpool Street station's glass canopy
over the Broadgate entrance.*

area of all, both for historic reasons and because of its density as London's trading hub, is Liverpool Street station. There, threading a very large new station through the existing tangle of underground infrastructure was monumentally challenging. And of course it yielded some remarkable archaeological finds going back to Roman times. In all these cases, the smooth movement of people using the line had to be carefully calculated and modelled – an aspect of architecture and design that is invisible. How many people will enter and leave the station, and by which entrance? How many will transfer under ground to other lines, existing or planned? Can conflicting flows be avoided? Can people disperse easily into the surroundings? What will be the likely impact of demographic change on movement patterns over time? It cannot be a precise science and the best precaution is to

Looking up from the foot of the escalators to the diamond patterned ceiling at Farringdon's western ticket hall.

over-provide circulation space at the outset along with multiple ways in and out, allowing for expansion such as space for extra escalators when needed.

But no matter how consistent you try to make your engineering and space/circulation planning, everywhere is different, even under ground. The benefit of this to us, the users of the system, is that a great deal of the architectural character of each station derives from the way each site is differently squeezed and built. There is, for instance, a dramatic double-back on your descent from the surface to a grand intermediate concourse at the Farringdon end – interchanging with the considerably upgraded north-south Thameslink rail service – which is designed with structures and finishes to reflect the jewellery district of Hatton Garden. It is very different at the smaller eastern exit, at the far end of Smithfield Market within view of the towers of the Barbican. There the architecture adapts in sympathy, with a lofty concrete toughness. Both ends serve the emerging City of London 'Culture Mile', which includes the Museum of London (transferring to the currently empty Smithfield Market at the Farringdon end) the Barbican and Guildhall School of Music and Drama, and a new home for the London Symphony Orchestra under Sir Simon Rattle to be built on the site being vacated

Tottenham Court Road western ticket hall concourse with its distinctive 'drum' ceiling-mounted light and acoustic fittings.

by the Museum of London. Given that the Moorgate end of Liverpool Street station also serves the Culture Mile, its public transport connections are about to improve radically.

Such station duality is repeated in the different circumstances of Tottenham Court Road – where the colour palette of the main eastern entrance is light, the smaller Soho entrance on Dean Street dark, but tied together by common elements such as the distinctive 'drum' ceiling-mounted light and acoustic fittings. Similarly at Bond Street the spacious Hanover Square end is very different in feel from the residential Davies Street end, though both ticket halls have a calm, modern-classical feel. Liverpool Street is more unified aesthetically at both ends (Moorgate and Broadgate) with its striking folded-plate ribbed surface treatments. Arguably it is a not dissimilar urban context at both ends, the financial quarter – but with the added cultural oomph of the Barbican just to its east as we've seen. In this way the four key central stations, each with station entrances at both ends, are effectively eight.

You'll notice the difference between the station types – the underground boxes and the deeper mined types. The grandeur of the rooms you move through from street to platform and back is especially apparent at Paddington (forecast to be the busiest station on the new line) and Canary Wharf. Box stations both, these are notable sequences of spaces, taking you down logically level by level but again, with very different treatments.

Tottenham Court Road
station, eastern ticket hall,
concourse level.

Platform level at Canary Wharf station.

Canary Wharf station.

Paddington has Brunel-inspired masonry with a glass canopy (and is designed to Brunel's imperial measurements). Canary Wharf has bright, gleaming surfaces including a transparent canary-yellow to the escalator sides – though it is mostly memorable for the roof of its retail 'oversite development' built over the station. This triangular laminated-timber structure is finished in inflated pillows of translucent ethylene tetrafluoroethylene, a lightweight fluropolymer. This glittering rocket-ship-in-a-dock, its nozzles serving the ventilation needs of the station 30 metres below, encloses a free-access rooftop garden with a restaurant at each end.

In contrast Woolwich is a shallower box station beneath new blocks of apartments and shops, but has a stately, broad portal onto a green in the former Arsenal site, with the façade detail derived from the metal-casting (and medal-casting) that used to take place in the foundries there. This south-east corner of London from here to Abbey Wood is where the Elizabeth line is having the greatest catalytic effect, stimulating an enormous amount of the new housing the capital needs as it expands downriver. The feel is distinctly different from the deeper mined stations of the central zone. These have a different aesthetic spatially as well as decoratively, with more of a sense

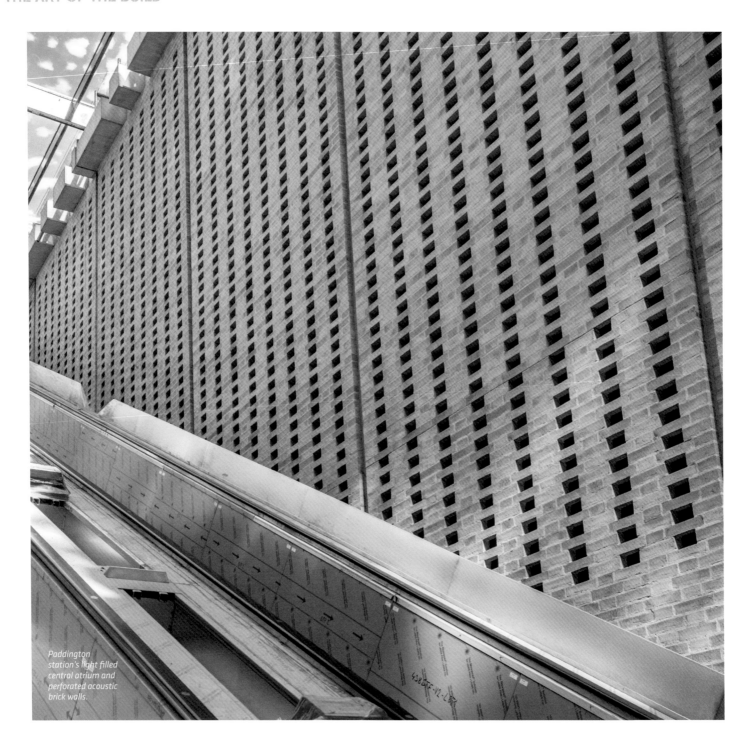

Paddington
station's light filled
central atrium and
perforated acoustic
brick walls.

Looking up at Spencer Finch's 'A Cloud Index' artwork on the glass canopy at Paddington station.

Custom House station was built in a narrow site between a road and the DLR.

of passing through a portal to a different world – or conversely emerging into different worlds, given their different ticket hall treatments.

There are also three absolute one-offs: Whitechapel, Custom House and Abbey Wood. Whitechapel was an especially difficult puzzle to solve with its existing Overground and Underground lines already interchanging close to the surface in a densely-packed part of town. Unpicking this resulted in a particularly ingenious design that also opens up the wider area, notably to the communities north of the station, with school and sports centre, which were previously cut off. The new ticket hall is made as a mezzanine bridge structure with a 'green' sedum roof supported from the sides of the historic deep brick-lined railway cutting below, letting daylight wash down its sides. Escalators down to the new Elizabeth line slice through the western vent shaft building. But none of this is apparent from Whitechapel's high street where the original station frontage is retained, with a much-widened pavement acting as forecourt.

Custom House, in the Royal Docks close to ExCeL London, is a long narrow two-storey above-ground station on a long narrow site, built of Nottinghamshire-made precast concrete parts in a post-and-beam frame that subtly skews to the angled road grid of its locale. Finally, Abbey Wood (also a surface station) is the only new terminus on the system, a timber-lined design with a swooping manta-ray roof that links its forecourt on a busy road bridge to the platforms below, with new landscaped public plazas to either side. It acts as a new civic focus for this fast-transforming area which includes Thamesmead. As with nearby Woolwich, it's an area which after suffering years of neglect is now coming sharply into focus as a key part of expanding residential London.

The narrow site for Custom House station meant the concourse had to be built out above the tracks.

The timber roofed
Abbey Wood station
ticket hall.

The proposed residential developement over the new station site at Woolwich in southeast London

Beyond the showpiece stations described here, a clutch of radically revamped stations west of Paddington (Ealing Broadway, Hayes & Harlington, West Drayton) are less grand affairs but also look promising. As with their equivalent stations on the east London and Essex branch of the line, it is as much the urban realm improvements carried out with local authorities (pedestrian squares and green landscaping) as the rebuilt or extended stations themselves. In total there will be 190,000 square metres of improved public space associated with the line with cycle parking, lighting and seating to enhance use of the space.

The new architecture of Crossrail is not strictly transport-related: the 'oversite' developments that fill in the gaps made by the city-centre worksites and help to pay for the line. They also often cunningly conceal the vent shafts and air-handling equipment of the system. London will thus close over the enormous holes dug, providing a variety of office, residential and retail buildings, even a new theatre at Tottenham Court Road. As we have seen, these dovetail with a set of wider landscape projects – the open surface spaces and green retreats to complement the enclosed spaces within and below. This is the first time that such a UK transport link has looked beyond its boundaries in this way.

The figures are revealing. There are 12 developments along the line plus the knock-on effect. That translates into planning consent for 90,600 homes by 2021, for instance (expected to double by 2026) plus an estimated 4.4 million square metres of office and retail floorspace as part of the legacy of the line. Then there is the general uplift in property values along its route. Surveys have shown that this uplift is clear up to a kilometre from the stations, and likely further. On the principle of the interwar 'Metro-Land', rapid rail links lead to increased demand and rapid building activity. Now this is all obviously beyond the remit and aesthetic control of the designers and builders of the Elizabeth line – though this wider impact was expected and planned for from the outset. In the central zone there has been necessary close collaboration with developers for the oversite commercial developments. The first and biggest of these at Tottenham Court Road was handed over to its developers in January 2018 and will re-make a strategic London crossroads complete with a new theatre and a public plaza next to the refurbished Centre Point tower. Crossrail 2 is also planned to run through here. No surprise that the combined regenerative impact is being felt right through Fitzrovia, Soho and Bloomsbury, and it's a similar story around Farringdon, Bond Street and Paddington.

London is forever rebuilding, but here we have a particularly concentrated series of interventions. As for the stations themselves, it is always hard to predict how a single large new public building will be received in use, let alone a whole string of them. And the experience is much more kinetic: one of movement, departure, arrival. We'll mostly spend more time in the Derby-built Class 345 Aventra trains than in each of these complex works of engineering, architecture and design. But they will become as familiar as our streets, squares and parks. They are anything but incidental: they are real, new, places, with ambition. And they will change the way we regard our city, as much as the way we use it.

The striking coloured design of North Woolwich portal headhouse.

The other architecture of Crossrail: the headhouses

A railway line can be defined as a string of buildings connected by shuttles full of people whizzing back and forth along ribbons of metal and concrete. Crossrail is no exception to this rule but when it comes to the buildings, there is more to be found than the signature stations with their sometimes multiple points of entry and exit. There is a second tier of architectural structures, equally vital though much less often used by us, the public. In fact in a perfect world we would not use them at all. These are generally described as the 'headhouses'. They can be in full view, or near-invisible.

At its simplest, a headhouse allows emergency evacuation if, say, trains were to become immobilised below ground between stations. Obviously they also allow access for maintenance, repair, security and fire-fighting teams. Crossrail's tunnels – much wider than Tube tunnels – are equipped with a continuous raised walkway on one side so that it's straightforward to evacuate trains should the need arise. In the central London section of the line where stations are relatively close together, you'd simply follow emergency exit signs to the nearest station – though there is a secondary access point at Fisher Street between Tottenham Court Road and Holborn which will be integrated with a new oversite building.

Most of these headhouses are in the outer tunnelled sections where it's further between stations – especially at points where the tunnels come to the surface. Where they pop up above ground they can form into clusters including other functions, such as pumphouses draining water out of the line, or electricity substations feeding power into the line. For instance out east

The eye-catching headhouse of Victoria Dock portal clad in multi-coloured vertical 'baguettes'.

The design of the Connaught Tunnel headhouse was drawn from the curving brick form, reminiscent of the old foot tunnel head houses.

The striking design of the Royal Dock headhouse, an electricity substation that feeds power into the line.

in the Limmo Peninsula where the River Lea meets the Thames near Canning Town, a large Crossrail worksite with access shafts will disappear beneath residential development – but the headhouse and power supply building alongside will be there to see.

As you'd expect, security is tight and the headhouses typically sit within well-protected maintenance compounds. Where they are in plain sight, architecture plays its part – some of the architects being drawn from the same experienced roster who have designed the stations. There is a series of eye-catching headhouse buildings clad in multi-coloured vertical 'baguettes' of terracotta, for instance – by the tunnel portals at Royal Victoria Dock, North Woolwich and Plumstead. Another, by the Connaught Tunnel portal in the Royal Docks, takes a curving brick form, reminiscent of the old foot tunnel headhouses you find at Greenwich and Woolwich. It has a square companion. The Mile End Park headhouse takes a landscaped-mound form, with a curving retaining wall of brick.

As with much of Crossrail's construction, the shafts originally sunk to build the line perform a later function – either becoming parts of stations or, as here, providing the vertical access routes for the headhouses. Vent shafts with their enormous fan chambers are more often hidden in buildings in various ingenious ways. An exception is Paddington, where the ventilation equipment is housed very visibly in carefully-designed, temple-like rectangular pavilions sitting in the street.

"It all amounts to quite a lot of building, and we were looking to give a sense of visual continuity," says Julian Robinson, Crossrail's chief architect. *"The challenge was to make them as positive a contribution to the local environment as we could."*

LIVING BY THE LINE

Local residents share their thoughts about the
benefits of the new transport connections in their local area.

Malcolm Knight
Local resident, Abbey Wood

"The Elizabeth line is putting Abbey Wood on the map. The construction here has been exciting to watch. I visit the site every day to look at the works and take pictures. I now have over 8,000 photos that even the site teams use.

The quicker and easier connection to Paddington will mean I can use the train again to visit my son in Wiltshire. My Freedom Pass makes getting around London very affordable and the Elizabeth line will provide me with several new route possibilities which I am keen to explore."

"The Elizabeth line will be great for Londoners like me. It will be easier and quicker to get around everywhere. It will mean only one train and my journey to work will reduce from an hour to 20 minutes!

I work in at a bar just near the new station by Hanover Square. We are looking forward to the Bond Street station opening and increased passengers creating more of a local buzz."

Julija Jakaite
Works in the West End,
lives in Woolwich

Steven Ingall
Business owner,
West Ealing

"The Elizabeth line and the planned upgrades to West Ealing station will be the 'rebirth of west Ealing' and make it a destination again. The new line will help businesses like mine. It will enhance business and make it easier for us to get around and clients to come to us."

Janpal Basran
Local charity manager and resident, Southall

"Being on the TfL rail network will open up employment prospects and allow people to look for work in areas they hadn't previously considered. The quick links to central London will broaden the social and cultural opportunities for people here. This will also be an opportunity to promote the diverse community in Southall.

We are already seeing new investment coming into the area, such as programmes to improve health and wellbeing, where previously we would have been overlooked. I am looking forward to more investment and programmes coming in that will benefit and build our community."

Callum Hanslip
Local resident and travel
ambassador for people with
disabilities, Chadwell Heath

"Since the introduction
of the TfL Rail service
[precursor to the Elizabeth
line], station facilities such
as lifts have been more
reliable. The biggest change
has been the new trains.
They are more spacious,
they have increased my

independence and made it
easier for me to get around.'

I've definitely noticed new
shops and places to eat
opening up around the
station. It's been great
having more choice."

A LINE OF ART

Louisa Buck

The nine artists who have made public artworks for the new Elizabeth line stations are part of an illustrious history of art commissioned for London's underground stations. Right from the beginning, London Underground blazed a trail in working with the most significant artists, designers and craftspeople. From Edward Johnston's now–iconic round logo, registered as a trademark in 1917, to posters designed by Laszlo Moholy-Nagy in the 1930s or Eduardo Paolozzi's mosaics in Tottenham Court Road station, this pairing of the most advanced engineering with the most innovative artistic visions has enhanced the journeys of the travelling public for many generations. More recently TfL's Art on the Underground has continued to build on this legacy with a diverse programme of temporary and permanent art projects in all media by internationally renowned artists as well as those at the beginning of their careers.

The prominent presence given to art in each of the seven new central Elizabeth line stations designed and built by Crossrail builds upon the philosophy of putting art at the centre of the capital's transport system to enhance the passenger experience. In each case the artwork has been developed in synchronicity with the architecture of the building and never as an afterthought or bolt-on.

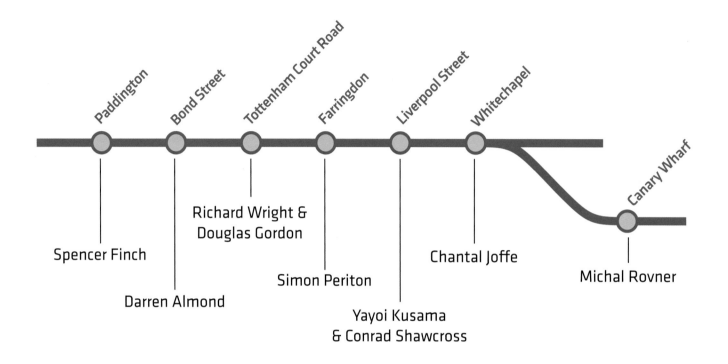

Crossrail commissions from Spencer Finch, Darren Almond, Douglas Gordon, Richard Wright, Simon Periton, Yayoi Kusama, Conrad Shawcross, Chantal Joffe and Michal Rovner have all been developed and conceived in close collaboration with Crossrail engineers and architects. The result is a series of works that are both physically and conceptually integrated into the fabric of each of the new underground stations, and often make a point of referencing aspects of the station's location within the city.

Crossrail's art programme may be an intrinsic part of this vast building and infrastructure project, but it has been funded separately by monies raised by the Crossrail Art Foundation, a registered charity founded with support from the City of London Corporation. Under the umbrella of the Crossrail Art Foundation, each of the seven stations has its artworks funded by an individual corporate sponsor, with match funding provided by the City of London Corporation.

Identifying and selecting artists of a suitable calibre was a similarly multi-stranded process which involved working with both the commercial and public sectors of what has become an evermore complex and interconnected art world. In a reflection of London's role as an international art centre,

*Sample artworks on display
at Whitechapel Gallery.*

FARRINGDON STATION

each new station was partnered with a leading and often local gallery who, in collaboration with Crossrail's art team, drew up an initial longlist from the artists they represented (the exception to this was Whitechapel station whose long list was made in association with the Whitechapel Gallery). Next, specialist panels made up of independent curators and art experts as well as Crossrail representatives, whittled these down to a shortlist of three to four artists per station. These artists were approached to develop a proposal in close association with the station architects and the panel selected the final project to progress.

The result is a series of artworks that brilliantly and inventively rise to the challenge of negotiating the many elements and stakeholders that make up this massive building and infrastructure project. Not only does Crossrail's public art programme enrich our experience of the new Elizabeth line stations but it also explores how they function as social and cultural environments as well as transport hubs. In short, this major act of patronage matches the ambition of London's newest railway line and the wide range of communities it serves.

SPENCER FINCH
'A Cloud Index'
Paddington station

Sponsor: Heathrow & City of London Corporation
Gallery partner: Lisson Gallery

Spencer Finch is known for making sculptural installations that blend the scientific and the poetic in an attempt to capture the experience of natural phenomena. Shifting effects of light, colour and atmosphere are key preoccupations, as are the act of seeing and the specifics of a place.

All these concerns are expressed in the artificial cloudscape that Finch has created for the roof canopy at Paddington station. In 'A Cloud Index' pastel drawings of clouds, made by Finch, have been massively enlarged and digitally replicated in white ceramic frit paint across 180 glass panels. These cover an expanse longer than a football field and 2,300 square metres in total.

"I like that it is very big but that it also has a light touch. The artwork is totally integrated into the station and into the purpose of the glazing of the canopy, as there would have had to have been some sort of diffusing pattern or it would have been too bright. So it ended up serving the dual purpose of creating an artwork and also reducing the glare."
Spencer Finch

19th century English romantic landscape painting was a key inspiration and most particularly John Constable's obsession with recording clouds at different times of the day and year. Constable called this process 'Skying' and it often took place not far from Paddington, on Hampstead Heath. Finch's giant cloudy canopy also recalls the proximity of Isambard Kingdom Brunel's original Paddington station and the memory of the steam trains that it served.

Finch's meticulously observed 'A Cloud Index' pays tribute to a British tradition of cloud classification by presenting a taxonomy of thirty seven different cloud types that would never naturally appear together at the same time. His is a man-made sky. This graded canopy which progresses from the chunkiest cumulo nimbus through to the lightest of whispy cirrus interacts with the real clouds outside, bathing the station in an ever-changing show of light and shadow. It is a glorious paradox that a phenomenon as immaterial and ephemeral as a cloud has its essence captured in a work so permanent and monumental.

"The artwork will exist both as an artificial cloudscape and as a homage to the British obsession with categorising and systematising the most fugitive of natural phenomena. Since Luke Howard first created a nomenclature for clouds in 1803, the efforts to comprehend and quantify clouds have been both beautiful and quixotic, and clouds always seem to stay one step ahead of human understanding."
Spencer Finch

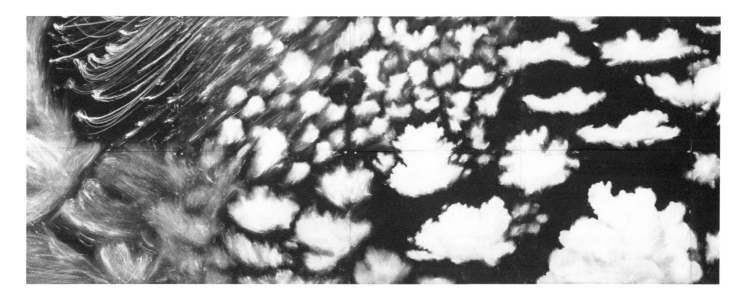

(Above) Early pastel sketches
for 'A Cloud Index'.
(left) Progress photography of
the 120 metre long canopy on
Eastbourne Terrace.

'A Cloud Index'
at Paddington
station.

DARREN ALMOND
'Horizon', 'Train of Thought' and 'Timeline'
Bond Street station, western ticket hall

Sponsors: Selfridges & City of London Corporation
Gallery partner: White Cube

Time and travel are central preoccupations of Darren Almond. Fully functioning digital clocks, bus stops and trains have featured prominently in his films, paintings and photographs, as part of an ongoing exploration of the physical and psychological experience of time and place. As a child Almond was a keen trainspotter with an early awareness of clocks and timetables and the way in which the language of numbers and numerical systems parcel out time and regulate every aspect of our everyday life continues to be an enduring theme. In form and style the three projects for Bond Street resemble the embossed metal nameplates that were affixed to early British locomotives, but here they have been greatly enlarged and cast in aluminium or bronze and bear very different forms of information. They are all made by the same heritage sign company who made many of the boilerplates for locomotives of the past.

'Horizon' is positioned over the main escalators in the entrance hall of Bond Street station and presents travellers with an abstract field of fragmented numbers which emerge from a rectangular mosaic grid of 144 aluminium panels. Cast in relief and highly polished, these incomplete disjointed digits cascade below a 'horizon line' made up of grouped half numbers, their tumbling trajectory echoing the descent of travellers to the platforms below. The only complete figure is a zero which pokes above the massed numerical horizon to denote either a sunset or a sunrise. As the work faces towards the east Almond errs towards the optimism of a sunrise. Jumbled partial numbers carry connotations of hectic schedules and daily routines but Almond also hopes that the piece will offer a brief pause for contemplation for station users as they embark upon their journeys.

"Before you've even physically begun a journey you are already thinking in a numerical language: the first question we all ask ourselves is, 'What time is the train?' So it seemed appropriate to mark the starting point of the journey with a work engaged with a similar language."
Darren Almond

Over the entrance to the lower escalator to the Elizabeth line Almond has installed a giant sign that reads 'Reflect from Your Shadow', a phrase that evokes a sense of departure and leaving something in your wake. Almond has used this nameplate format in earlier sculptures which substitute train names for poetic phrases, recalling both his own trainspotting days as well as the golden age of the British railways. Succinct but complex, the text is intended to provoke thought rather than be instantly understood.

"Reflect from your shadow serves as an ever-changing point of reference. It is at once an affirmation of existence and a guide to help forge a clearer path. It asks you to consider your experience before making judgment and to consider what you leave in your wake, both at a personal and collective level. It highlights who we are and where we are: without light there would be no shadow."
Darren Almond

'Timeline' presents another evocative phrase, 'From Under the Glacier', divided up into a sequence of four single word plates, this time cast in icy silver aluminium. Designed to be viewed as you begin your ascent to the surface, it is a powerful reminder of the physical reality of Crossrail's deep subterranean tunnelling and the way in which station users are journeying through millennia of geological time as they ascend to the streets above. Glaciers are believed to have reached as far south as London during the Ice Age.

"We are in those strata and literally coming up from under the glacier. What could be more dramatic than to be reminded that your physical presence here, at this very point, is only made possible by passing through geological time itself?"
Darren Almond

REFLECT FROM YOUR SHADOW

'Train of Thought', highlights who we are and where we are: without light there would be no shadow. The nameplate format has been used in earlier sculptures which substitute train names for poetic phrases.

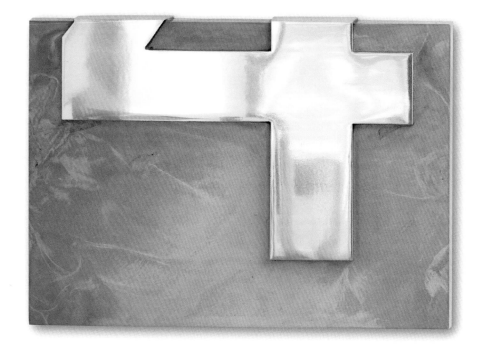

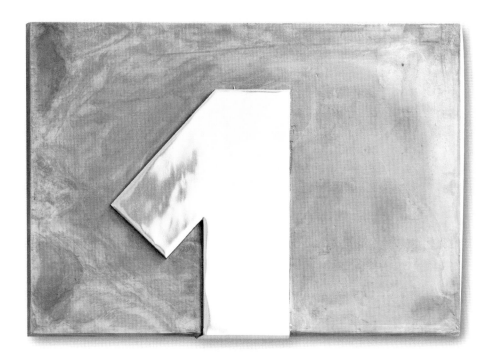

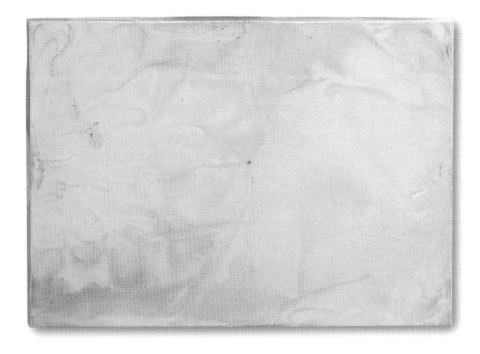

Samples of 'Horizon'.
The artwork is a grid of 144 aluminium panels.
Cast in relief these incomplete disjointed digits
cascade below a 'horizon line' made up of grouped
half numbers. They are all made by the same
company that made many of the boilerplates for
locomotives of the past.

DOUGLAS GORDON
'Non-Stop'
Tottenham Court Road station, western ticket hall

Sponsors: Almacantar, City of London Corporation & Derwent London
Gallery partner: Gagosian

Douglas Gordon remembers wandering around the streets of Soho when he first came to London to study at the Slade School of Art in the late 1980s. Although enticed by the neon signs of the neighbourhood's bars and strip clubs, he was too nervous to go in. It is this experience of the young boy from Glasgow who was drawn to the forbidden fruit of what went on behind the closed doors of the city's centre for bohemian bad behaviour that has inspired 'Non-Stop,' his film work for the western Dean Street ticket hall at Tottenham Court Road underground station. The giant eye that blinks from a giant screen above the escalators in the western ticket hall is Gordon's own and the signs that are reflected on his retina are those of Soho establishments that no longer exist. When installed, as it beams out into the street outside, the film will also become a beguiling siren sign in its own right.

"I used to walk around that neighbourhood as a wee Scotsman only looking at things from the outside – because I was too nervous to go in – and this is again what makes it perfect for me is that I am revisiting something from my past – something I didn't experience. I always wanted to see it – but I never got in – so the eye is my desire to look, look, look."
Douglas Gordon

For more than two decades Gordon has been making work – often using the moving image – that investigates memory and human experience. An early work listed every person that he could remember meeting up to the year of 1990, another presented a playlist of thirty pop songs all released during the time of his mother's pregnancy that he might have heard in utero. The role of the moving image in shaping the human imagination is repeatedly explored, and his most famous work is still probably '24 Hour Psycho' (1993), which slowed down the Hitchcock classic to last an entire day. Another memorable early film 'The Divided Self' (1996) presented two arms, one smooth, the other hairy, both locked in equal combat and each the artist's own. 'Non-Stop' marks another grapple with desire and its denial.

"When you get out into the public you need to think of yourself as public. This is maybe one of the most political works I've done. It's about getting into London and also getting out of London and the fact that I was a temporary Londoner who now lives between Glasgow, Berlin and Paris. It's an essential part of my memory and I hope it will make people reflect on where they are."
Douglas Gordon

Now Soho is in a state of change with the Elizabeth line a key part of its transformation. But Gordon insists that his film is not so much an exercise in nostalgia as more of a 'DNA profile' of the streets surrounding Tottenham Court Road station. With this most visceral homage to his old stamping ground the artist is also paying tribute to the many multitudes of all nationalities who carry Soho as part of their personal histories, as well as to those who will do so in the future.

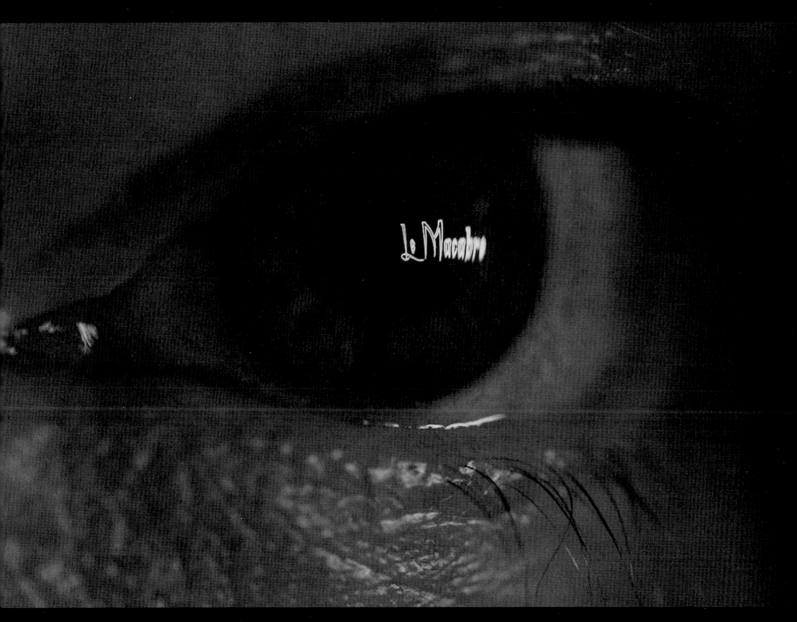

Film still from the pre-production of
the artwork 'Non-Stop', 2018.

(Right) Richard and his team
applying the design to the ceiling.
(below) Concept illustration of the gold
leaf artwork in place on the concrete
ceiling above the escalator shaft.

RICHARD WRIGHT
no title, 2018
Tottenham Court Road station, eastern ticket hall

Sponsors: Almacantar, City of London Corporation & Derwent London
Gallery partner: Gagosian

Richard Wright makes intricate abstract wall paintings which transform interior spaces. They can cover entire walls, ceilings or stairwells or be found in less conspicuous corners and even on the floor. Sometimes minimal, sometimes highly elaborate, these works are always unique and made in direct response to their setting. Wright considers not only the architecture of a site but also what he has described as the 'symptoms' of a space: the quality of its light, its history, location and atmosphere. His sources are many and various, ranging across art history, graphics and typography but are always developed intuitively according to the site. Most of Wright's works have an intentionally brief lifetime and are made to be viewed for a finite period before being painted over. The Crossrail project is therefore a comparative rarity being one of only a few pieces that he has created to remain in perpetuity.

For the eastern ticket hall of the Elizabeth line at Tottenham Court Road station, Wright has mapped out an intricate geometric system in gold leaf on the concrete ceiling above the escalator shaft. This is based on continuous intersecting lines in which the uniformity is at times interrupted and adapted to provide different perspectives and spatial illusions when viewed from various vantage points as travellers move through the space. The starting point was the conventional types of tiling that are to be found across many metro systems but here the design is as much about animated surface, space and visual play.

"I'm hoping that it will provide a moment of preoccupation or delay and perhaps out of your peripheral vision you might engage with this place, this space."
Richard Wright

Like all Wright's work, his Crossrail painting has been laboriously made using medieval and renaissance fresco techniques whereby a paper drawing is pierced with thousands of holes through which fine powder – or in this case watercolour – is rubbed to create faint outlines on the walls. Once the whole image is on the ceiling each part of the design is hand-gilded, artisan style, by Wright and his team applying sheets of 24 carat gold leaf directly to the concrete surface and using a natural glue to hold the leaves in place. Wright especially likes the physical qualities of gold and the way in which, although one of the most stable of materials, its appearance is in a constant state of flux. Depending on the light, gleaming shininess can shift to an opaque black or seem almost to disappear altogether. In the airy white glass and stainless steel of Tottenham Court Road's eastern ticket hall all these qualities will be brought into full effect.

"Gold has this immateriality, a quality of being absent and present and at the same time. It appears and disappears, it is almost not there at all."
Richard Wright

(Right) Early stage of the ornate hand-gilded ceiling at Tottenham Court Road. Created by Richard Wright and his team applying sheets of 24 carat gold leaf directly to the concrete surface.

SIMON PERITON
Farringdon station
Western ticket hall: 'Avalanche'
Eastern ticket hall: 'Spectre'

Sponsors: Goldman Sachs International & City of London Corporation
Gallery partner: Sadie Coles HQ

Simon Periton's earliest works were elaborate cut out paper works that subverted the genteel patterns of the lacey doily with anarchist symbols and images from punk, psychedelia and pop art.

One of the last paper cutouts that Periton made was based on a diamond structure and this was the starting point for his sequence of enormous gems that tumble down and along the interior walls of Farringdon's western ticket hall. Digitally printed in dark grey ceramic ink onto back-lit glass panels up to three metres tall, they have an ominous glamour, their intricate shard-like facets are highlighted in vivid pinks, greens and yellows so that they shimmer and appear three dimensional. Periton's cascading frieze of punkish precious stones echoes the dynamism of a busy station peopled by travellers in perpetual motion. They also make reference to the history of the site with nearby Hatton Garden renowned for centuries as London's diamond district and the centre of the UK jewellery trade.

At the same time, Periton also considers these fragmented mineral forms to be a reminder that in order to use the station, travellers are also journeying through London's subterranean geological strata. He sees it as a happy coincidence that the diamond shapes formed by the station's roof trusses are echoed in the angular structures of his gems, further integrating them into their surroundings.

"The work will be experienced in glimpses and that's where a public artwork is different to putting a piece in a gallery...it will be observed for smaller amounts of time but more regularly, so it's a completely different viewing experience."
Simon Periton

Periton's second artwork for Farringdon faces outwards. An elaborate curvaceous pattern has been printed in pale grey onto the exterior glazing that runs around three sides of the building. The design is based on a drawing by the Victorian botanist, theorist and designer Christopher Dresser titled 'Force and Energy' and dated between 1867-73. Dresser's drawing almost directly coincides with the building of Smithfield meat market which is situated directly opposite the station. In its curling sinuous organic forms, Periton's intricate glazing acknowledges the ornamental 19th century metalwork of the market as well as deliberately referring to the etched glass to be found in Victorian pubs. With exuberance and delicacy it throws shadows into the ticket hall and frames the view outside.

"Visually the content of the piece was exactly what I was after in terms of the organic feel for the building but also its timescale was almost exactly the same as when Smithfield was built, so it seemed to be the perfect coming-together of something organic but also structured by mankind."
Simon Periton

(Above) Prototype testing of the illuminated designs for 'Avalanche'.
(right) Detail of artwork design for 'Avalanche'.

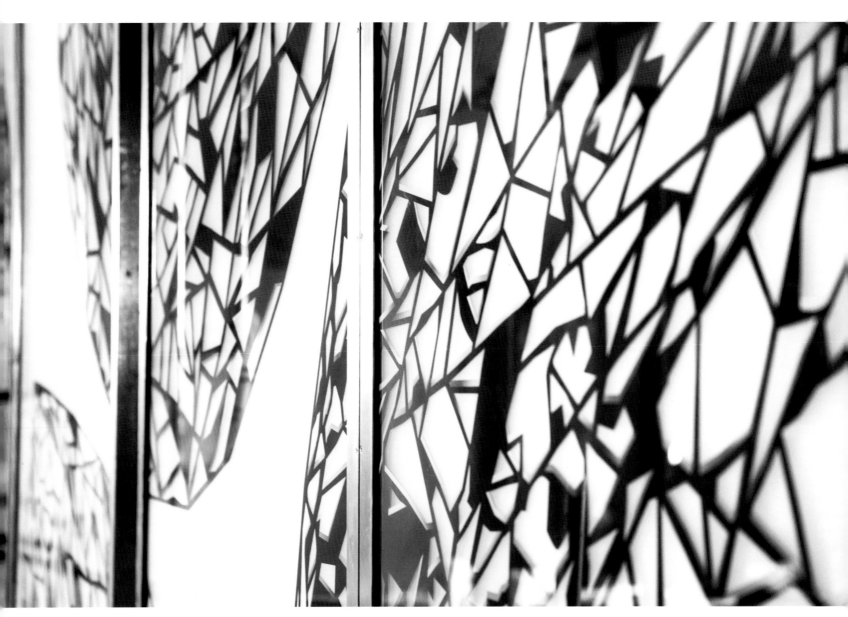

(Above) Detail of 'Avalanche' installed in
the western ticket hall.

(Above) Detail of 'Spectre' installed in the eastern ticket hall.
(left) The design for 'Spectre' was inspired by a sketch by the Victorian botanist, theorist and designer Christopher Dresser titled 'Force and Energy' and dated between 1867-73.

ELIZABETH LINE

MOORGATE STATION

Concept illustration of 'Manifold (Major Third) 5:4' in the public realm outside the Moorgate entrance.

CONRAD SHAWCROSS
'Manifold (Major Third) 5:4'
Liverpool Street station, western ticket hall

Sponsors: Landsec & City of London Corporation
Gallery partner: Victoria Miro

Complex ideas from science, mathematics, philosophy and history are all integral to the sculpture of Conrad Shawcross. Inspired by a range of technologies and natural forces, his work can take the form of elaborate machines or intricate structures based on geometric systems. It is often epic in scale. For the public space outside the Elizabeth line entrance to Liverpool Street and Moorgate station, Shawcross has drawn on his ongoing interest in harmonics and the mathematics of music to create Manifold (Major Third) 5:4. This bronze sculpture renders sound as image by giving three-dimensional form to the third chord in the harmonic spectrum, also known as the 'major third'.

Conrad first visualised this chord by using a machine based on a Victorian harmonograph. Its two swinging pendulums – one attached to a pen, the other a piece of paper – recorded the oscillations of its sound waves, here in the ratio of 5:4. In Shawcross' specially modified device, the paper pulls through in the manner of ticker tape or an electrocardiogram machine, and so captures the diminishment of the chord over time, going from loops to a flat line. The marks yielded by this process then formed the preliminary sketches to be realised in Manifold's three dimensional tree-like form with its crown of energetic loops, all of which coalesce into a single vertical stem that descends directly into the ground.

"It is a picture of a chord falling into silence. It begins its life as this feverish spinning whirlwind and when it gets slower, it gets fatter as the energy in the system dissipates down into the stem which peacefully goes into the ground."
Conrad Shawcross

While Manifold openly owes its existence to the specifics of mathematics and harmonics, it also offers a rich range of poetic and metaphysical readings. The word itself means 'many' or 'numerous', with the notion of folds, both inwards and outwards also literally expressed in the sculpture. Manifold also refers specifically to the part in a combustion engine which merges the exhaust gases from multiple cylinders down to one single pipe in what Shawcross describes as 'a beautiful, tendril-like organic form.' Similar qualities are shared by his sculpture of the same name and its intricate intestinal tangle provides an animatedly curvaceous counterpoint to the rigidly angular geometric façade of the new Liverpool Street station. Yet while appearances may differ, both the organic-looking sculpture and the building are equally reliant on numerical systems and ratios.

Cast in bronze in many hollow sections which have then been welded together and polished into a unified whole, Manifold is an intricate piece of engineering which wears its monumentality lightly. Its footprint may be tiny, but its scope and impact is anything but.

"It doesn't have to be seen as a musical chord – people may see it as an tornado or a diagram of the wind, but I don't want it to be seen as in any way arbitrary. All the modeling is very constrained and specific to a particular thing and I hope that this comes across in its rigour."
Conrad Shawcross

YAYOI KUSAMA
'Infinite Accumulation'
Liverpool Street station, eastern ticket hall

Sponsors: British Land & City of London Corporation
Gallery Partner: Victoria Miro

Japanese artist Yayoi Kusama is best known for her use of massed repetitive polka dots which first emerged in her work in the 1950s and have become one of her signature motifs. Covering the surfaces of her paintings and sculpture and often swarming over every element of her all-encompassing multi-media installations, these multitudinous spots carry many meanings for the artist. For Kusama they express both the underlying unity as well as the instability of the cosmos and our often precarious place within it.

"The moon, the sun, each and every star, my life, your life: they are all a single polka dot among billions."
Yayoi Kusama

In 'Infinite Accumulation' Kusama's trademark dots have evolved into steel spheres linked and supported by undulating curvilinear metal rods to form flowing arrangements in three dimensional space. In the past Kusama has used similar elements in a series of smaller wall-mounted sculptures, but never before on this scale or for permanent public installation. Configured into four separate sequences, the gleaming silver orbs hover above the ground and are highly polished to reflect everything around them. The positioning of these suspended spheres and the swooping serpentine arcs that connect them have been conceived to interact with the public space around the eastern entrance to Liverpool Street station and they provide a fluid animated response to the surrounding architecture. The dynamism of the piece is also the result of Kusama intuitively hand-twisting the wires holding up the balls on the original models.

For Kusama, this most engaging of public sculptures expresses both the individual and the collective within the urban landscape. Echoing both the organic and the other-wordly it invites everyone who encounters it to respond to and connect with their environment in new and unexpected ways.

"London is a massive metropolis with people of all cultures moving constantly. The spheres symbolise unique personalities while the supporting curvilinear lines allow us to imagine an underpinning social structure."
Yayoi Kusama

Yayoi Kusama's
'Infinite Accumulation'.

(Above) A panel of 'A Sunday Afternoon in
Whitechapel' in fabrication.

(right) One of Chantal Joffe's original
portrait collages for the series.

CHANTAL JOFFE
'A Sunday Afternoon in Whitechapel'
Whitechapel station

Sponsors: City of London Corporation with grants from Art Fund and Randeree Charitable Trust
Gallery partner: Whitechapel Gallery

Chantal Joffe often spends her Sundays in the streets and markets around Whitechapel station, having lived in east London for many years. Her two-metre tall portraits on the east and westbound platform walls of the Elizabeth line station were inspired by the cosmopolitan throng observed on these weekend wanderings in her local neighbourhood, an area that has also been home to London's migrant communities for centuries.

"Whitechapel is a vivid, beautiful diverse area that's full of people and with an incredible atmosphere. It's why I love London."
Chantal Joffe

On-the-spot records of individuals that caught her eye were the starting point for a series of small paper collages which distill the distinguishing features of each passer-by into simple shapes and colours. Joffe then worked with fabricators to enlarge and reproduce these snipped shapes into sheets of laser-cut aluminum without losing the hand made 'drawn with scissors' quality of the originals or the liveliness and individuality of her subjects. It was important that the metal sheets were thin enough to be stacked and layered to create the composite figures using the same method as the paper versions. So they are monumental in scale but still carry the lightness of their making.

Joffe is known for making psychologically complex figure paintings but here she chose the cut-out format for its bright, graphic clarity and its instant ability to communicate. Her aim was to humanise a bustling, impersonal public space and to make people feel more at home by forging an instant personal connection with these unknown but familiar individuals, in much the same way that we might weave stories about the fellow travellers that we see on our daily commute.

"All my thinking around this project has been about the journeys we make and how we make them our own – through the people we see on a daily basis, or the private maps of significant places we carry in our heads. Part of the challenge has been to develop small intimate collages into large scale works and to retain a sense of the personal in a public space."
Chantal Joffe

'A Sunday Afternoon in Whitechapel' pays homage to Seurat's 'A Sunday Afternoon on the Island of La Grande Jatte' (1884) which depicts Parisians relaxing on the banks of the Seine. Likewise Joffe presents us with the full multigenerational, multicultural spectrum of east Londoners at leisure, and in doing so celebrates the vivacity of urban life in the streets above and around Whitechapel station.

"I like the idea of creating an identity for the station which is a very beautiful architectural space, and I wanted the art in it to link the under ground with the above ground and the sense of Whitechapel as a bustling inner city place with a hospital and a market. It was really important that you feel that aliveness and I wanted you to feel very strongly, I know where this is: this is Whitechapel."
Chantal Joffe

MICHAL ROVNER
'Transitions'
Canary Wharf station

Sponsor: Canary Wharf Group plc & City of London Corporation
Gallery partner: PACE

Michal Rovner originally studied cinema, film and photography and in the past has collaborated with the filmmaker Robert Frank and the composer Philip Glass. Although her work can take many forms she is best known for working with film and video to depict crowds of people and sometimes birds and animals in order to address universal issues of history, identity, memory and place.

At Canary Wharf, a large video screen installed at the station entrance features repeated rows of her characteristic silhouetted figures which move along different levels of horizontal and slanted lines in a composition inspired by the dramatic architecture of the station, its escalators, platforms and passageways. Every so often these armies of humanoids cross each other, come to an abrupt halt and then shunt off again, resembling trains arriving and departing from the station platforms. Some of these lines of tiny figures are silhouetted in black, most are in white as they glide back and forth, stopping and starting against a shadowy atmospheric backdrop made up of landmark buildings from the London skyline.

In their state of perpetual motion, Rovner's ghostly throng both echoes and reflects the restless dynamism of Canary Wharf station. It also reminds us of the tides of humanity that course and flow through London, a vast metropolis whose lifeblood has always been people moving from place to place.

"I've always been fascinated by human movement in time and in space and the continuous flow of people passing from one place to another. The composition of my work is inspired by the architecture of the place and the different levels and the different vectors of movement."
Michal Rovner

They may be abstracted down to the point where they lose all individuality, but Rovner regards this interconnected spectral multitude as an affirmation rather than a denial of humanity.

The thousands of people that she depicts in her works are not artificial constructs but real individuals, each of whom was originally filmed by Rovner personally. After this face to face encounter with her crowds she then digitally removes all identifying features so that, by losing the specifics of their age, race and gender, these indistinct bodies represent all or any of us. They could be you or me.

"I hope that my work in this place, seen by millions of people, will remind them that the time that they take for granted, going from one place to another, and the space between, is actually very meaningful. By coming here and moving from one place to another, they are part of the magical human flow in time."
Michal Rovner

Concept designs for
the digital artwork
installation by Michal
Rovner.

THE ARTISTS OF THE PROJECT

SPENCER FINCH

Born: 1962, New Haven, Connecticut, United States; Lives and works in New York
Education: Hamilton College, Doshisha University, Rhode Island School of Design

Spencer Finch is best known for ethereal light installations that visualise his experience of natural phenomena. His investigations into the nature of light, colour, memory and perception proceed in watercolours, drawings, video and photographs.

DARREN ALMOND

Born: 1971, Appley Bridge; Lives and works in London
Education: Winchester School of Art

Darren Almond uses sculpture, film, painting and photography, and real-time satellite broadcast to explore the effects of time on the individual and nature. Harnessing the symbolic and emotional potential of objects, places and situations, he produces works which have universal as well as personal resonances.

RICHARD WRIGHT

Born: 1960, London; Lives and works in Nottingham
Education: Edinburgh College of Art, Glasgow School of Art

Richard Wright is best known for his site-specific yet transient works that unite painting with graphic and typographic elements, charging architectural spaces with a fourth dimension of subtle optical complexity. Alongside metal-leaf schemes on walls and ceilings, Wright's works on paper encompass a range of handmade prints, ink drawings, gilding, and watercolours. Wright was awarded the Turner Prize in 2009.

DOUGLAS GORDON

Born: 1966, Glasgow; Lives and works in Berlin, Germany
Education: 1984–88, Glasgow School of Art; Slade School of Fine Art, London, 1988–90

Douglas Gordon is best known for his films and large-scale video installations, often using 'found' material. His practice encompasses a diverse body of work spanning narrative video and film, sound, photographic objects, and texts. He won the Turner Prize in 1996, the Premio 2000 at the 47th Venice Biennale in 1997 and the Hugo Boss Prize in 1998.

SIMON PERITON

Born: 1964, Kent; Lives and works in Bath
Education: 1990, St Martin's School of Art

Simon Periton makes intricate cut-outs, often marked by an an elaborate and sensuous style. From his earliest paper 'doily' sculptures, Periton has embraced a breadth of historical influences – from nineteenth-century aestheticism to punk and anarchism. He typically invokes kitsch subjects and styles, only to subvert and complicate them through a mesh of competing references. His recent works have frequently combined 2D and 3D forms in unexpected ways, playing with ideas of surface versus depth.

CONRAD SHAWCROSS

Born: 1977, London; Lives and works in London
Education: 2001: MFA, Slade School of Art, University College, London; 1999: BA, Fine Art, Ruskin School of Art, Oxford

Imbued with an appearance of scientific rationality, Conrad Shawcross' sculptures explore subjects on the borders of geometry, philosophy, physics and metaphysics.

Throughout his career Shawcross has experimented with ideal geometries and topologies; these constructions are conceived as systems which could be theoretically extended infinitely into space.

YAYOI KUSAMA

Born: 1929, in Matsumoto-shi, Nagano-ken, Japan; Lives and works in Japan
Education: 1948-51 Studied at the Arts and Crafts School, Kyoto; 1957-58 Studied at the Art Students' League, New York.

Yayoi Kusama has developed a practice which resists any singular classification. Since the mid-1960s Kusama's artistic endeavours have spanned painting, drawing, collage, sculpture, performance, film, printmaking, installation and environmental art as well as literature, fashion and product design. Kusama's work – often incorporating polka dots or pumpkin motifs – is far-reaching, expansive and immersive.

CHANTAL JOFFE

Born: 1969, St Albans, Vermont, United States; Lives and works in London
Education: 1992–94: M.A. Fine Art, Royal College of Art, London; 1988–91: BA (Hons) Fine Art, Glasgow School of Art

Chantal Joffe is known for her insightful contribution to the genre of figurative art. Almost always depicting women or girls, sometimes in groups but recently in iconic portraits, Joffe's paintings, often appropriating existing imagery, distort

MICHAL ROVNER

Born: 1957, Israel; Lives and works in Israel and New York City
Education: 1979–81, Tel Aviv University, Cinema/Television and Philosophy; 1981–85, Bezalel Academy of Art, BFA

Michal Rovner uses video, photography and sculpture to express conflict, the cyclical nature of history, dislocation and human interaction. Her work is stripped of any narrative or people with distinguishable features, creating new and immersive worlds.

THE IMPACT OF CROSSRAIL

Tony Travers

The Elizabeth line will add 10% to central London's rail capacity. This fact alone gives a clue to the importance of the project to the city's future. In the 150 or so years since the first underground railway opened from Paddington to Farringdon, no single project will have had such physical and symbolic importance for the city.

Bazalgette's sewers may still be the single most important engineering project ever delivered for London, but there can be little doubt that the Crossrail project will similarly be remembered as a great leap forward for the capital's infrastructure.

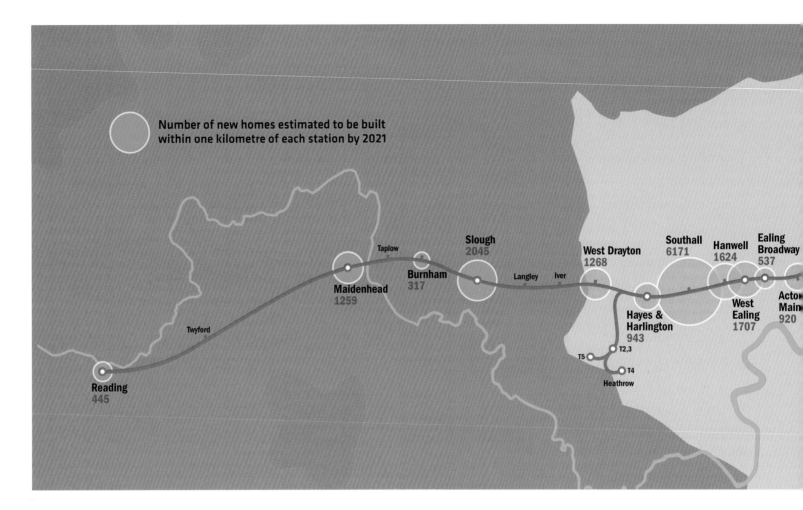

Number of new homes estimated to be built within one kilometre of each station by 2021

Reading 445
Twyford
Maidenhead 1259
Taplow
Burnham 317
Slough 2045
Langley
Iver
West Drayton 1268
Heathrow T5 T2,3 T4
Hayes & Harlington 943
Southall 6171
Hanwell 1624
West Ealing 1707
Ealing Broadway 537
Acton Main 920

The scale of change

A single railway project that adds 10% to the rail capacity of the central area of a city with a massive existing rail system is indeed remarkable. London has one of the world's most extensive and comprehensive railway networks. The familiarity of the Tube map and its 'London's railways' spin-offs make it possible to take for granted the sheer scale of the network.

The line runs east-west and will therefore have most obvious immediate impact between its Shenfield and Reading end-points. Places that were an hour or more from each other will now be significantly closer. The expanding property markets around outer London stations such as Ilford and Hanwell already attest to the transformative power of a frequent, high-capacity, rail link.

The line will open at a time when outer London is anyway going through a property development boom because of a cyclical shift of price-advantage from inner to outer boroughs. There is capacity for large numbers of new homes in the relatively

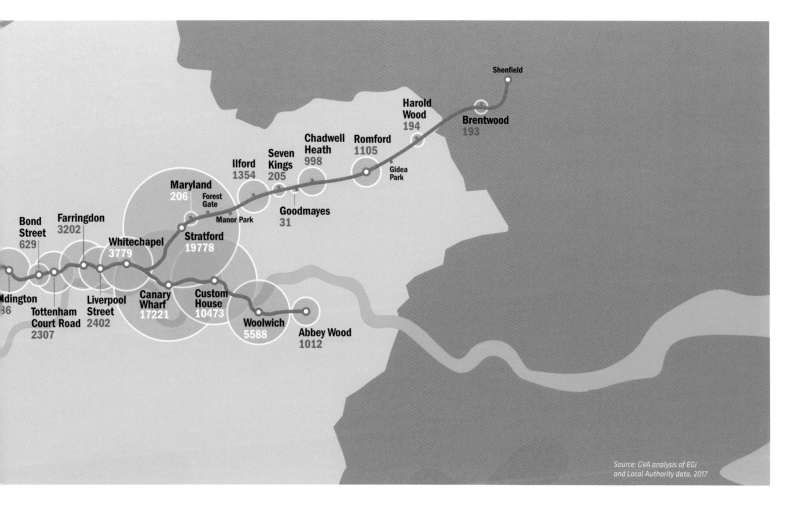

Shenfield

Harold
Wood
194

Brentwood
193

Chadwell
Heath
998

Romford
1105

Seven
Kings
205

Ilford
1354

Gidea
Park

Maryland
206

Forest
Gate

Goodmayes
31

Manor Park

Bond
Street
629

Farringdon
3202

Whitechapel
3779

Stratford
19778

ddington
6

Tottenham
Court Road
2307

Liverpool
Street
2402

Canary
Wharf
17221

Custom
House
10473

Woolwich
5588

Abbey Wood
1012

Source: GVA analysis of EGi
and Local Authority data, 2017

lower density area between inner London and the green belt. Most outer boroughs and the Mayor of London wish to increase house building. The added connectivity brought by the new railway will open up far more sites than would otherwise have been the case. Current analysis shows more than 90,000 new homes are already planned along the route for completion by 2021, 66% of which cited Crossrail in their planning. This expands to a predicted 180,000 by 2026.

In the short term, the new service will also take pressure off the Underground's Central line and, to a lesser extent, other lines with an element of east-west capacity. Larger stations at Farringdon, Tottenham Court Road and Paddington will reduce crowding there, but also in places such as Holborn and Oxford Circus.

The land-use and transport impacts should together open up a 118 kilometre long corridor of development across the

largest urban economy in Europe. The key question raised by such potential is how far local authorities and their residents are prepared to allow a significant increase in activity. At many points along the line there has traditionally been powerful opposition to additional development. Heritage and conservation considerations have added to the difficulties faced by developers. Thus, the amount of Crossrail-related development in central London has so far been limited to redevelopment within existing property volumes. The full economic impact of the project will to a large extent depend on the extent to which the planning system is able to deliver bigger (not necessarily taller) development along the line.

London's growth

The Elizabeth line in its completed form has been mooted since the Central London Rail Study (CLRS) in 1989, though British Rail had suggested something similar in 1980 and proposals for other routes across the city go back further still. At that time, London's population was 6.6 million, down from 8.6 million in 1939. The CLRS was commissioned because of a sharp and unexpected increase in rail demand in London and the South East. This increase, it turned out, was a leading indicator of population growth from 6.6 million in the late 1980s to approaching nine million by 2019 when the Elizabeth line fully opens. That being the case, London will have a population a third larger when the railway is fully open than when it was originally proposed.

This scale of increase is the equivalent of adding the populations of Birmingham, Leeds and Manchester to London within 30 years. Put another way, justifications for Crossrail in 1989 were on the basis of a population well below that of 2019. Costs, of course, turned out to be higher than those of 1989. Governments may wish to consider the implications of the fact that delay to major projects will almost always add to their cost. But looking forward from the opening of the line, what impacts is it likely to have on the city's future?

Existing projections already suggest London's population is likely to grow to well above nine million. No one can yet know what impact Brexit will have on longer-term UK economic growth, migration and broader openness. Because London is a prosperous gateway from the rest of the world to the whole of the UK any impacts, negative or positive, are likely to be most immediately felt in the London region. Other impacts, such as changes to the international labour market, may affect London more profoundly even than Brexit.

New Class 345 trains on test near Prince Regent station, East London.

Crossrail and the rest of the country

The Crossrail project has required the purchase of expertise and materials from across the UK. Estimates suggest that around 15,000 jobs were created and a further 55,000 supported in the supply-chain generated by the project, with 62% of them outside London: the rolling stock which will run east-west across the capital was built in Derby; the reinforced concrete panels which clad central stations was manufactured in Doncaster. The project is regional rather than local to London and the benefits have been spread across the UK.

All UK cities need improved public transport if they are to compete with those elsewhere in the world. Trams and improved heavy rail lines are being delivered in Greater Manchester, Birmingham/West Midlands and other city regions. Importantly, the delivery of the project has proved important in stimulating other parts of the country to press for improved city transit systems.

What next after Crossrail?

Within a year or so of the Elizabeth line opening, the Thameslink project will be delivered, offering a peak time 24-train per hour service north-south across London and intersecting with its cousin Elizabeth line at Farringdon. Together, the two projects will mark a radical leap-forward for the city's transport system. A lobby to take Crossrail 2 forward has been in place for some years now.

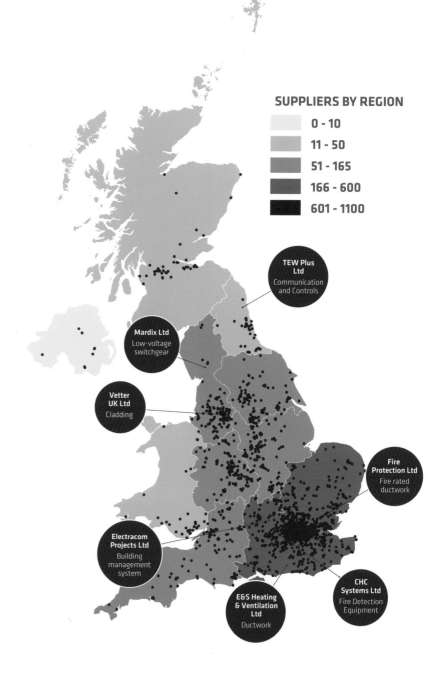

SUPPLIERS BY REGION

	0 - 10
	11 - 50
	51 - 165
	166 - 600
	601 - 1100

TEW Plus Ltd
Communication and Controls

Mardix Ltd
Low-voltage switchgear

Vetter UK Ltd
Cladding

Fire Protection Ltd
Fire rated ductwork

Electracom Projects Ltd
Building management system

CHC Systems Ltd
Fire Detection Equipment

E&S Heating & Ventilation Ltd
Ductwork

Metalwork from
Northern Ireland was
used on the project

High Speed Two (HS2), the government-sponsored national railway line from London to Birmingham and then Manchester and Leeds, will deliver substantial additional passengers at Euston, creating demand for improved travel southbound across central London from 2026. Crossrail 2 would link north east of the capital (through Enfield and Haringey) to south west London, via Euston and Tottenham Court Road. The latter would be a key intersection for the two Crossrail lines.

However, the government has signalled that Crossrail 2 will have to be financed in such a way that a significant part of the immediate construction costs are paid for by contributions from within London itself. HS2, by contrast, will be fully funded by the national taxpayer. The challenge of putting together a package that will meet the government's demands risks delaying the start of the next phase in increasing the city's transport capacity.

Transport for London also has plans to extend the Bakerloo line along the Old Kent Road and on to Lewisham, with a potential second phase to extend further. Funding will be tough for this line too, given central government signalling that other parts of the UK, notably the Northern Powerhouse, are to be given greater prominence in future years. These investment decisions need to balance the need for capacity against the opportunity for growth and the competing priorities for funding. There are many compelling cases.

London, Brexit and the next five years

The UK's decision to leave the EU will have profound impacts on the economy for a number of years to come. London, as the most international part of the country, might expect to see a particular effect, though the government's own estimates suggest the capital will be less affected than all other regions. Certainly the flexibility of London's vast private sector is likely to make it easier for its economy to adjust to conditions outside the EU.

In the two years since the Brexit vote, London's population and employment have continued to grow strongly. The conditions which created the demands for the Elizabeth line appear still to be in place, though medium-term impacts on the city's economic and population growth should not be taken for granted. An ill-conceived Brexit settlement, however brought about, could have the effect – at least temporarily – of reducing demand for public transport. A smooth transition to a new trading world could see London's growth sustained.

The city's longer-term future

In the longer-term, London is likely to see its population grow towards 10 million, with a regional ('wider south east') population of perhaps 15 million more, producing a total of over 25 million. The scale of activity within this broader region means it would continue to be one of the largest regional economies in the world, comparable with the New York-New Jersey region and Tokyo-Yokohama. Over time, other mega-city regions will catch up, though it seems unlikely that London would drop out of the top league.

The additional capacity added to London's transport in 2018-19 will encourage further development and economic growth. Railways have proved a remarkably durable form of mass public transport in cities. Even if autonomous vehicles change travel patterns in outer London, the need for high-capacity services to the centre will surely remain important.

Cities will be used increasingly for leisure as well as high-productivity work. The Elizabeth line will celebrate its 25th anniversary in December 2043, by which time it is plausible to assume that Crossrail 2 will be open, with the, as yet unimagined, Crossrail 3 project being prepared. Railways, the Victorians' gift to posterity, look set to thrive into the middle of the 21st century and beyond.

A new Class 345 train in Paddington mainline station.

FOCUS ON

Suppliers across the country have been involved in building the Elizabeth line.

CONTINUING DESIGN TRADITION

A. J. Wells & Sons Ltd, The Isle of Wight

A medium-sized enterprise located on the Isle of Wight, A.J. Wells is among three companies manufacturing signage for the new Elizabeth line stations. Inside their workshop are three generations of experience and knowledge gained from producing iconic vitreous enamel signage for TfL and London Underground.

For this project, they utilised a wide range of in-house manufacturing capabilities and have worked with suppliers across the country to create the roundels and wayfinding signage for Tottenham Court Road, Farringdon and Whitechapel stations.

To meet the challenging requirements of the brief, they developed specialist glass panels and unique slimline light patches to allow for even illumination in the different station environments, without the use of plastics. The finished product, now installed in all the new Elizabeth line station sites, will add a contemporary feel to Transport for London's 110-year-old design.

BRIDGING THE GAP

Cleveland Bridge, Darlington

Cleveland Bridge's structures cross some of the world's great rivers and waterways, connecting countries and bringing communities together. Their structural achievements are architectural icons that have transformed the skylines of many cities.

It was one such stucture that has become a new photographic icon at Canary Wharf's Elizabeth line station. The link bridge and elevated walkway – which forms part of the access into the new station.

Tapping into over 150 years of engineering skill, the elevated walkway was built as a steel framework which sat on three sets of tubular legs and bearings at both ends of the walkway. The legs were supplied in two halves and had to be carefully aligned and then welded into position on site.

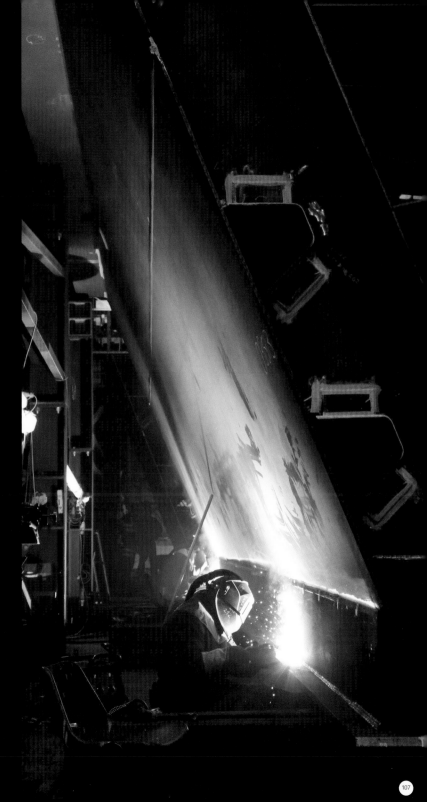

BRIGHT FUNCTIONAL ARCHITECTURE

Independent Glass, Glasgow

The Glasgow-based company responsible for manufacturing glass panels that line the ticket hall walls at Tottenham Court Road station has years of specialist experience working on production and supply of toughened, laminated safety glass products for all types of rail projects.

For the Crossrail project, they have manufactured a series of red, white and black glass panels, which are on average 2.5 metres high by 1.5 metres wide, using state-of-the-art machinery that enables the production of materials of such large proportions. On each panel they have digitally printed a dot-matrix design which represents an abstracted grid map of Soho.

The coloured glass will be used to help passengers identify the different areas of the station and play on the contrasting local characters at each end. Black glass will be used in the western ticket hall and white in the east. Red walls will be seen in the lower concourse of the eastern ticket hall as passengers make their way to either the Elizabeth line or the Northern line platforms.

PROVIDING SUPPORTS

Environmental Fabrications, Dromore, Near Belfast

Based in Dromore, Northern Ireland, Environmental Fabrications employs over 50 personnel within its purpose built factory.

The company has provided 300 tonnes of steel to Crossrail. They have supplied access platforms and handrails to sites in east London and Kent and fitted gantry cranes and provided additional structural supporting steel for jetties to help with the transport of concrete segments used to line the new rail tunnels.

Their work on the project has played a significant part in helping the company pick up more work across the country.

AHEAD OF THE CURVE

GRC UK, Doncaster

Within an industrial estate, south of Doncaster is GRC UK – the manufacturers of bespoke glass-fibre reinforced concrete (GFRC) panelling that cover the walls of Tottenham Court Road, Liverpool Street and Whitechapel. The beautifully curved GFRC panels for the mined Elizabeth line stations will give a distinct and spacious feel that is a result of an architectural vision to celebrate the geometry of the tunnels.

The company has used the scale of the Crossrail project and the custom cladding design as an opportunity to introduce technology and software not traditionally used in construction. Digital modelling software and a robotic milling machine were used to create the moulds that helped produce double curvature concrete panels in their various forms.

The panels were created using a mix of glass fibres added to a concrete slurry, a process that allows the cladding to be both lightweight and robust. Due to the high fibre content, the cement slurry and fibres are applied directly to the mould surface using a spray technique. This is a highly skilled operation and is only manufactured by specialist GFRC producers.

In the open-plan, light-filled factory 29,000 panels have been produced from 2,300 moulds, each element carefully hand-finished before being installed.

TRAINS FOR THE FUTURE

Bombardier Transportation, Derby

Working in conjunction with the team at Transport for London, Bombardier has led the design and build for the 70, nine carriage, 200 metre long trains that will carry 200 million passengers annually on the Elizabeth line.

The trains have been designed to be 25% lighter than existing trains on the network and have energy-efficient features such as aerodynamic design, smart software that maximises energy recovery during braking and smart sensors that help manage cooling, heating and air flow.

Once the train is on the production line, the efficient process of assembly includes welding and painting pre-fabricated parts, interior fit-out, door installation, high pressure water testing (for leaks), and connecting the bogies. Testing in the workshop and then on the test track for operational trials follows. Each train requires roughly 70 days for production led by teams of skilled engineers and apprentices.

The £1 billion contract is supporting 760 UK manufacturing jobs and 80 apprenticeships.

The new 345 trains will be
housed in the specially created
Old Oak Common depot.

Julian Glover

Julian Glover is a journalist and writer.

Author of the best-selling biography *Man of Iron: Thomas Telford and the Building of Britain* (Bloomsbury), he is leading a review into the future of National Parks for the Government.

Associate Editor of the London Evening Standard, he was previously a columnist for *The Guardian*.

In 2011 he was appointed chief speechwriter to David Cameron before being made special adviser to the UK Department of Transport, where he worked with a range of projects including Crossrail.

 Hugh Pearman

Hugh Pearman is a London-based architecture and design critic. He edits the *RIBA Journal* and contributes to many other media ranging from the *Sunday Times* – where he was architecture critic for 30 years – to *The Spectator*, *Royal Academy Magazine*, *V&A Magazine*, *Icon* and, in the United States, *Architectural Record*. His books include the bestselling *Contemporary World Architecture* (Phaidon).

An Honorary Fellow of the Royal Institute of British Architects, Hugh has also served as a vice-president of London's Architectural Association. In 2015 Hugh was Visiting Professor in Architecture at the Royal College of Art.

 Louisa Buck

Louisa Buck is a London based writer and broadcaster on contemporary art. She is London Contemporary Art Correspondent for *The Art Newspaper* and a regular reviewer for BBC Radio 4's Front Row and BBC World Service. She writes a bi-weekly visual arts column for *Telegraph Luxury*, and contributes to many other publications ranging from *Vogue* to *Art Quarterly*, *The Guardian* and *W Magazine*.

She is the author of a number of catalogue essays for institutions including Tate, Whitechapel Gallery, ICA London and the Stedelijk Museum in Amsterdam. Her books include *Commissioning Contemporary Art: A Handbook for Curators, Collectors and Artists* (Thames & Hudson).

Louisa is a visiting lecturer at Sotheby's Institute and was a judge for the 2005 Turner Prize.

 Tony Travers

Tony Travers is director of LSE London, a research centre at the London School of Economics. He is also a professor in the LSE's Government Department. His key research interests include public finance and local, regional and London government.

He has chaired the London Finance Commission, been a member of the City Growth Commission and been advisor to the House of Commons Education Select Committee and Communities and Local Government Select Committee.

An Honorary Member of the Chartered Institute of Public Finance & Accountancy and also of the Institute of Revenues, Rating & Valuation, he has published a number of books on cities and government including *London's Boroughs at 50* (Biteback Publishing).

Credits and acknowledgements

In the production of this book we would like to thank colleagues at Crossrail, its supply chain and delivery partners.

All images are © Crossrail, unless otherwise noted, and in particular we would like to acknowledge the work of James O'Jenkins and John Zammit.

Page 15 - Images of Brunel's engine shed at Paddington Yard. Great Western Railway Trust

Page 20 - Victoria line train. © TfL from the London Transport Museum collection.

Page 73 - Film still from Non Stop. © Studio lost but found / VG Bild-Kunst, Bonn 2018

Page 103 - Class 345 train. © TfL from the London Transport Museum collection.

Thank you to our principal sponsor

Bechtel is part of the integrated management team on Crossrail. Along with Systra and Halcrow (a CH2M company) Bechtel is employed as the Project Delivery Partner for the central 21 kilometres twin tunnel section and eight new stations from Paddington through Canary Wharf to the southeast and through Pudding Mill Lane to the northeast. Bechtel is also the delivery partner for Network Rail and its extensive Crossrail programme to upgrade the existing rail network.

Since 1898, Bechtel have completed more than 25,000 extraordinary projects across 160 countries on all seven continents. They operate through four global businesses: Infrastructure; Nuclear, Security & Environmental; Oil, Gas & Chemicals; and Mining & Metals.

With grateful thanks to

The Arup Atkins JV led the design for Tottenham Court Road, Custom House and Woolwich Elizabeth line stations and the 42 kilometres central section tunnels. As well as designing the tunnels, the team undertook impact assessments on over 18,000 buildings, railway substructures, utilities, and other assets adjacent to the route to see how they would respond to tunnel construction. Arup also designed Canary Wharf station, and worked for the Contractors at Liverpool Street and Bond Street stations. Atkins, in partnership with Grimshaw and GIA Equation, designed the station common architectural components to create an integrated line-wide identity, and worked for the contractor at Farringdon station.

Costain, the smart infrastructure solutions company, has provided engineering, complex delivery and commissioning services through the delivery phase on Crossrail. Costain engineers, programme managers and other specialists have supported Crossrail both as a principal contractor and through joint ventures. The Costain contributions to the completion of the Elizabeth line included designing and implementing the UK's first ever use of robotics for installing rail systems in tunnels, upgrading the Anglia connection between Stratford and Shenfield, and a leading role in delivering the new Paddington station Elizabeth line platform complex, including its passenger tunnel connection to the Bakerloo line. For over 150 years, Costain has been shaping the world in which we live. Our purpose is to improve lives by working with our clients and supply chain to increase the capacity, enhance efficiency and customer services of the UK's transportation, energy and water infrastructures.

London First has been galvanising business support for Crossrail since we started out in the early '90s. We campaigned loudly on the UK-wide economic benefits and championed a mixed-funding package, supported by business. We're now building on these successes to drive Crossrail 2 forwards. Our taskforce, chaired by Lord Adonis made a clear case for the scheme in 2013, and we're feeding into the government's affordable funding review due later in 2018. With the prize of 200,000 new jobs and homes and a big boost to GDP, the business stands firmly behind Crossrail 2 and just like we did for Crossrail, we'll be championing it all the way.

M M MOTT MACDONALD

Global engineering, management and development consultancy Mott MacDonald worked on eight of the 24 design contracts, including leading-edge tunnelling, station, signalling, power, ventilation and safety systems design, and specifications for rolling stock, materials and workmanship. Innovations for Crossrail include the construction of one of the largest caverns in London at Stepney Green, use of GIS systems for excavation control and spray concrete lining techniques. The consultancy also provided detailed design of Liverpool Street station and Paddington Integrated Project. This covered all aspects such as civil, structural, architectural, mechanical and electrical as well as construction planning, passenger and transport modelling, and rail safety assurance.

At Otis, we're dedicated to moving people. Our work on Crossrail is our latest contribution to London's transport system. We installed the first public escalator in Earl's Court Station in 1911 and are installing escalators for the Elizabeth line. Our customers look to us for new ways to keep their world moving. We are inventing the next generation of lifts with embedded intelligence to deliver a superior experience. Alongside new equipment installations, our national network of over 600 service engineers offers the highest levels of personalised service. We are proud to be a part of the team keeping the city moving.

OTIS

SYSTRA supports Crossrail as part of the Project Delivery Partner (PDP) team with Bechtel and CH2M. The company provides expertise in Railway Systems, Operations, Civil and Tunnelling Engineering for the 42 kilometres of tunnels and nine new stations. The SYSTRA group operates globally, with SNCF and RATP as major shareholders. It has 6,200 staff worldwide, providing engineering services, consultancy and transport planning in over 150 countries. In the UK SYSTRA has circa 400 staff across thirteen offices.

SYSTRA

The Transcend joint venture, comprising AECOM, Jacobs and The Nichols Group has been Programme Partner for Crossrail since 2009. Working as part of an integrated management team, Transcend implemented a collaborative and efficient programme management solution. Transcend's new products included baseline and master change control, Innovate18 and realisation of complex systems integration. We designed and delivered Innovate18, a world-class innovation-sharing platform shared between the Crossrail programme and its suppliers. Innovate18 generated many new ideas for enhancing technical capability during the delivery of Crossrail.

Transcend

WSP provides technical expertise and strategic advice in the property and buildings, transportation and infrastructure, environment, industry, resources and power and energy sectors. They have designed Bond Street station with an integrated multi-disciplinary team of engineers, architects, town, traffic and construction planners, cost managers and environmentalists. The design integrates into the confined surroundings of Mayfair and two constrained ticket hall sites. The method and sequence of construction has been an integral part of the design process including the oversite developments where we are the structural engineer for Great Portland Estates at Hanover Square. We are also working at Tottenham Court Road, Paddington, Farringdon and Abbey Wood on behalf of contractors, and elsewhere providing specialist Engineering Safety Management and RAM analysis support.